VOLCANOES

Passion and Fury

Text and Photographs by
Stephen James O'Meara and Donna Donovan-O'Meara

SKY PUBLISHING
Cambridge, Massachusetts

I have no room in my thoughts for anything but volcanoes, and it will be so for some days to come.

—Isabella L. Bird, *Six Months in the Sandwich Islands*

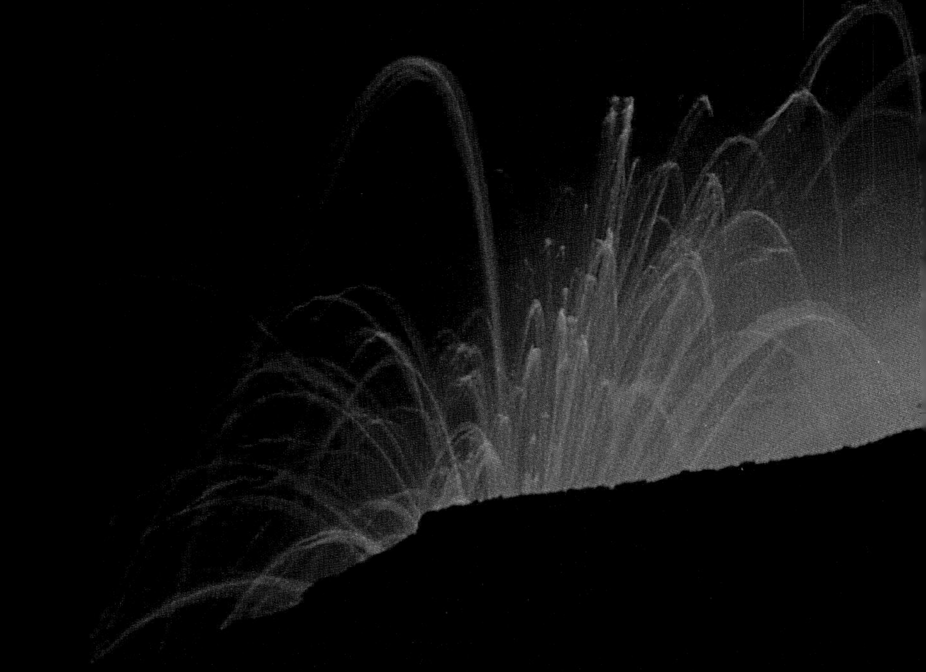

TOSSED RED-HOT CINDERS DRAW GRACEFUL ARCS AGAINST THE TWILIGHT. LAVA FLEEING TO THE SEA THROUGH AN UNDERGROUND TUBE IGNITES THIS JULY 1992 FIREWORKS DISPLAY OFF HAWAII'S SOUTHEAST COAST. SOME FRAGMENTS LAND IN THE OCEAN WITH A COMMEMORATIVE HISS.

Published by:

Sky Publishing Corp.
49 Bay State Rd.
Cambridge, MA 02138-1200

Library of Congress Cataloging-in-Publication Data

O'Meara, Stephen James, 1956–
Volcanoes : passion and fury / text and photographs by Stephen James O'Meara and Donna Donovan-O'Meara.
p. cm.
Includes bibliographical references (p. –)
ISBN 0-933346-70-0 (acid-free)
1. Volcanoes I. Donovan-O'Meara, Donna, 1954– II. Title.
QE521.3.044 1994
552.2'1—dc20 93-47387

Printed in Hong Kong

94 95 96 97 98 8 7 6 5 4 3 2 1

IN MEMORY OF

Jon Erickson, Voice of Hawaii's Volcanoes and a good friend.

Maurice and Katia Krafft, whom we never had the pleasure of meeting but who have inspired us to pursue our dreams and our passion for volcanoes.

All the courageous women and men who have lost their lives in the study of volcanoes.

Acknowledgments

There's no such thing as a lonesome traveler, because on any road there are always good people who offer kind words, helpful advice, and heartfelt companionship. We have encountered many such individuals in our journeys. Notably, we would like to extend a worldwide thank you to the directors and geologists of the volcano observatories: especially Franco Barberi, Sonia Calvari, and Rosanna Velardita in Sicily; Jean-Baptiste, Jeannette, and Luc Morel in France; Otoniel Matias and Eddy Sanchez in Guatemala; Raymundo S. Punongbayan in the Philippines; and Jack Lockwood and Thomas Wright in Hawaii.

Special thanks also go out to our volcano friends Edwin Aguirre, William and Anne Albrecht, Dick Ashbaker, Rolando Benítez, Edgar Castro, Peter Collins, S. René Evans, Anthony Irvine, Imelda Joson, Maxine Kaluna, Harry Kim, David H. Levy and L. Bean, Alfredo MacKenney, David Okita, Pele-Hiiaka of Volcano (our faithful but temperamental Pomeranian), and Dorian Weisel.

We'd also like to express our gratitude to Ann M. Castucci and Virginia Roth for their invaluable travel assistance, Forrest M. Mims III and Larry Steckler for their spiritual support of our adventures, as well as the beautiful people of Hawaii and all of those who lent friendship without offering us their names.

A deep bow goes to Edward A. Venzke of the Smithsonian Institution's Global Volcanism Network for reviewing our manuscript, Steve Peters for encouraging our book idea, Nina Barron for her careful and considerate editing, and Mary Santa Maria-Pietrowski for her elegant design. We are grateful to you all. Naturally, we accept complete responsibility for our prose and the facts it contains.

Finally, we appreciate the volcanoes and their gods or goddesses for tolerating our presence.

Like a genie freed from its earthen bottle, a fabulous steam cloud rushes away from tourists huddled on Hawaii's black lava cliffs. Nearby the ocean boils, bubbles, and pops. Lava rushing out of a submerged hole in the cliff enters the sea beneath the surface.

On Hawaii's Kilauea volcano a roaring lava fountain rises above Pu'u 'O'o vent. Golden rockets of liquid rock streak out of the crater, twist and twirl in the updraft, then fall to earth as crimson rain. When our tiny Cessna nears the fountain the temperature inside the plane's cabin sharply rises; the windows are almost too hot to touch. We feel as though we're approaching the fiery surface of the sun. This fountain is 245 meters high.

Contents

INTRODUCTION

ON OCTOBER 6, 1987, we exchanged wedding vows before an erupting volcano. After a year of making travel plans and seeking permissions we flew away from the beehive of Boston, Massachusetts, and headed for the most humble of earth's volcanoes, Kilauea on the Big Island of Hawaii. We must have looked strange wearing Victorian wedding attire and sneakers among the island's giant ferns and steaming volcanic fissures. David Okita, our pilot and best man, helped us to board his helicopter and, as requested, removed our door for a better view. He whisked us up and over the volcano's yawning mouth and then off to Kupaianaha, a molten lava lake boiling on the volcano's southeast slope. Beyond the lake's fuming cliffs, David skillfully lowered the helicopter to within 20 meters of a pumping mass of scarlet liquid rock. Hot, sulfurous winds blew into the cabin. The intense heat baked our skin as we leaned out to toss a dozen calla lilies into the lake as an offering to Pele, the Hawaiian goddess of volcanoes. A wave of lava folded over the large white flowers and quickly devoured them.

The wedding ceremony occurred in the shadow of a nearby active volcanic cone called Pu'u 'O'o (POO-oo OH-oh). There, on a field of newly fallen cinder — a spot of earth untouched by humankind — we dedicated ourselves to volcanoes as much as to each other. Since 1979 volcanoes had enticed us with their beauty and fire. Now we made them the driving passion in our new life together.

This book is about our experiences with volcanoes. We have visited many, 19 of which are shown here in some of their moods; these same moods inspired us to create the poetry that opens each section. A few volcanoes are old friends; others are relatively new

---

DREADLOCKS OF STEAM FLOW DOWNWIND OF MAUNA ULU, A SMALL SHIELD VOLCANO ON KILAUEA. BORN FROM A CRACK IN THE EARTH IN 1969, MAUNA ULU GREW 100 METERS BEFORE IT STOPPED ERUPTING FIVE YEARS LATER. NOW THE MAGMA BENEATH THE MOUNTAIN IS RECEDING, CAUSING THE CRATER'S FLOOR TO SINK AND ITS WALLS TO FRACTURE AND COLLAPSE. (HAWAII)

acquaintances. Each has a dynamic personality: when erupting, Kilauea can be as fluid as the hula; Mount Pinatubo in the Philippines is virtually unapproachable, putting on a godlike air and demanding only reverence; and then there's childlike Pacaya in Guatemala, acting strong and bossy, insisting on having its own way in its own world.

Born of fire, volcanoes are, in a sense, children of the earth. Those spotlighted in this book still draw life from their Mother Earth to survive. How wonderful it is that a volcano may awaken in one century, sleep through two, then return to life in ashen splendor. In this way volcanoes progress through time and become an intimate part of human culture. Underscoring this are the ancient myths and legends associated with volcanoes, morsels of which we have scattered throughout the book. For us to smell the acrid aroma of sulfur, hear the earth hissing from a crack, and see the glowing orange eye of a lava skylight is to enjoy what our ancestors once feared.

Their phenomenal beauty notwithstanding, all volcanoes are dangerous. Every year people around the world — even seasoned geologists and photographers — are hurt or lose their lives in eruptions. Despite precautions, we've been burned, cut, and bruised by lava. We've survived volcanic quicksand at Mount Pinatubo, acidic vapors at Poás in Costa Rica, and flying volcanic shrapnel at Kilauea. This book can be viewed as a risk-free way to "travel" to these venerable yet temperamental mountains. We hope our photographs and words bring you not only the sights but also the sounds, smells, and emotions of being there. So with utmost respect we present to you the volcanoes we have known.

Myth, mystery,
Romance, destruction —
A volcano is all these things.

SILKY SMOOTH, A LAVA BUBBLE BREAKS THROUGH A SHELF OF NEW LAND ON HAWAII, THEN POPS ITS TOP WITH A PUFF. LAVA BUBBLES, LIKE THIS METER-WIDE ONE, FORM WHEN SEAWATER EVAPORATES BENEATH THIN LAVA STREAMS.

But what are cuts, bruises, fatigue, and singed eyelashes, in comparison with the awful sublimities I have witnessed to-day? . . . I feel as if the terrors of Kilauea would haunt me all my life and be the Nemesis of weak and tired hours.

—Isabella L. Bird, *Six Months in the Sandwich Islands*

WITH A THUNDEROUS ROAR A LAVA RIVER POURS INTO THE COLD PACIFIC OCEAN. THE COLLISION TOUCHES OFF A STEAM EXPLOSION THAT PULVERIZES THE LAVA AND LAUNCHES MOLTEN SHRAPNEL INTO THE AIR. A MYRIAD OF BLACKENED LAVA BOMBS WHISTLE OUT OF THE STEAM CLOUD AND LAND HELTER-SKELTER ON THE SHORELINE. (HAWAII)

Awakening

The senses awaken,
The body and spirit awaken,
An infant awakens,
The earth awakens.

AWAKENING

February 2, 1993*. A paradigm of symmetry, Mount Mayon in the Philippines steams quietly over the lush farmland it helped to create outside Legazpi City. Its long, trademark plume ripples above farmers tending their crops in the afternoon sun. On the volcano's stark, upper slopes several hikers challenge themselves by climbing to Mayon's summit. Nature seems in balance. Then, without warning, Mayon erupts. In one horrible moment, the mountain hurls a menacingly dark ash cloud, shaped like a head of blackened cauliflower, some 4 kilometers into the sky. Gravity tugs on the heavy column, and it collapses. A gray avalanche of superheated debris rushes down the mountain with astonishing speed. In eerie silence the cloud envelops 75 people; they are instantly incinerated in the 1,500° Celsius heat. Thousands more flee as ash falls like snow 9 kilometers away. Thirty minutes later the mountain returns to sleep. Its first eruption in almost 10 years has ended in catastrophe.*

VOLCANOES ARE PREHISTORIC mountains living in the present. Their life cycles cannot be measured by human time scales. A volcano can sleep for hundreds or thousands of years — even appear dead — until, one day, it stirs. Millions of tons of rock begin to convulse. Stone lips open, and the mountain exhales hot, steamy breaths. Molten rock and gases far below the surface begin a race upward, pressing, oozing, and squeezing through cracks deep in the earth.

Sometimes molten rock can sneak surprisingly close to the surface without breaking free, like on the Big Island of Hawaii, where magma may be only a few thousand meters beneath the surface of Kilauea volcano. Then there are the reservoirs that hide beneath spectacular natural phenomena, like the geysers in Yellowstone National Park; Old Faithful performs in the throat

---

DESPITE ITS TRANQUIL APPEARANCE, MOUNT MAYON IN THE PHILIPPINES IS A KILLER. HERE, ONE MONTH AFTER IT FIRST ERUPTED IN 1993, LIGHT GRAY ASH MIXES WITH STEAM IN THE CRATER'S THROAT. THE BROWNISH SCAR AT THE BASE OF THE VOLCANO (AT RIGHT) IS WHERE A HOT ASH FLOW TOOK THE LIVES OF 75 FILIPINOS. THIS SCORCHED LAND IS KNOWN LOCALLY AS THE KILLING FIELDS. (LUZON ISLAND)

of an enormous, ancient, and active volcano whose water is heated by a molten mass some 10 kilometers underground. Still other volcanoes, like Vulcano near Sicily, leak enticing but dangerous yellow and blue sulfurous vapors that condense and crystallize around vents like delicate flakes of topaz snow.

When an eruption is imminent earthquakes occur more frequently and move closer to the surface. The ground swells until the molten rock and gases pressing against it break free. This could last minutes — or years. The men and women who study volcanoes can monitor only a handful of the thousands of potentially dangerous ones. In some developing countries, where countless people live on and near active volcanoes, the population relies on less scientific methods to anticipate impending eruptions: well water dries up, mammals and reptiles higher up migrate to the volcano's lower slopes, the volcano fumes more vigorously, white steam turns gray, rockslides increase, and at night the crater glows.

A volcano could display these warnings for days, months, or years before it erupts. Or, as with Mount Mayon, it can show no obvious signs at all. When will a volcano erupt? No one knows.

LIKE A LEGENDARY DRAGON AWAKENING, A TINY SKYLIGHT ON KILAUEA VOLCANO EXPOSES A FIERY EYE THROUGH SCALES OF PAHOEHOE LAVA. LAVA COURSING THROUGH A ROCKY TUBE JUST UNDERFOOT IS SEARCHING FOR A WAY OUT. A HOT BREATH RISES FROM THE OPENING AND WARMS THE AIR. (HAWAII)

Ocher plumes of acidic vapor tarnish the sun over Stromboli volcano. The devilish clouds descend on the volcano's summit, arousing raspy coughs from spectators (not shown) gathered there. Every 15 minutes the restless volcano stirs, firing a volley of molten grapeshot. (Lipari Islands, Italy)

A geyser in Yellowstone National Park, Wyoming, flips up a column of steam and sprays out a jet of water like a shaken can of soda. Ejected from a subterranean chamber, the water is heated to the boiling point by rocks overlying a deep magma reservoir. The park's 200-odd geysers (half of the world's total) reside in the immense 75-by-45-kilometer caldera of a prehistoric volcano that could erupt again, though probably not during our lifetimes. Interestingly, in 1985 – when this photograph was taken – strong, new thermal activity occurred on the caldera's eastern side, its youngest part.

Choked with lava and overdue for an eruption, Pu 'u 'O 'o vent on Kilauea volcano coughs up some molten phlegm. The ground under our feet trembles each time the magma surges. Our hearts pound in anticipation of an emerging fountain of fire. The 6-meter-high cone seen here formed after spatter had accumulated around the vent for days. Note the fine glass thread trailing an orange glob of lava at upper left. Such threads are known as Pele's hair. (Hawaii)

Behold the vestibule of hell. Two kilometers wide and 1,000 meters deep, the caldera of Mount Pinatubo displays the aftermath of one of the greatest volcanic events since the 1883 eruption of Indonesia's Krakatau, whose explosions were heard over 1/13 of the earth's surface and deposited ash on ships 6,000 kilometers away. As tranquil as Pinatubo's caldera appears, we should not be here, and the volcano lets us know. Explosion pits and steaming cinder cones jeer at our arrival. Powerful updrafts buffet the plane; it pitches and yaws like a leaf in the wind. A hot, sulfurous breath fills the cabin, and our interpreter all but faints. Hugging the ash-stained shore of a green lake stands the "devil's cathedral" — a dome some 600 meters wide of fresh, viscous lava rising out of the volcano's throat. To the aborigines, Mount Pinatubo is the home of Apo Namalyari (the one who creates), a god who looks over the spirits of their deceased ancestors. This dome, they say, is his black hair rising from the earth. Several hours later Mount Pinatubo ejects a thin ash plume. (Luzon Island, the Philippines)

WRAPPED IN A BLACK SHAWL OF CINDER, MACKENNEY CONE ON PACAYA VOLCANO NAPS BETWEEN ERUPTIONS. MEANWHILE, THE HURRICANE-FORCE WINDS AT THE SUMMIT COMPEL US TO SEEK SHELTER BEHIND A RING OF STONES. PACAYA HAS BEEN CONTINUALLY ACTIVE FOR NEARLY 30 YEARS. DURING OUR DAY-LONG VISIT, IT ERUPTED DOZENS OF TIMES. (GUATEMALA)

SEETHING SULFUR GASES EAT THROUGH THE CRUST OF VULCANO, SCRAWLING A BRILLIANT YELLOW SIGNATURE ACROSS CENTURY-OLD EJECTA. ALTHOUGH IT LOOKS ENCHANTING, THIS COLORFUL FUMAROLE EMITS STINGING, NOXIOUS VAPORS ABLE TO KILL A CARELESS ADMIRER. IT LIES ON A FRACTURED SECTION OF CRATER WALL INSIDE THE VOLCANO, WHERE THE CRUST IS HOT, FLAKY, AND INSECURE — ONE WRONG STEP COULD PLUNGE A FOOT INTO A POCKET OF 500°C GAS. THE LARGE BOULDER TO THE UPPER LEFT OF THIS VENT IS ABOUT THE SIZE OF A REFRIGERATOR. (LIPARI ISLANDS, ITALY)

IN MAY 1992 THE GASES ESCAPING FROM POÁS VOLCANO (OPPOSITE PAGE) WERE EXTREMELY ACIDIC. PERIODIC MISTS OF SULFURIC ACID ENVELOPED THE SUMMIT. HOLES IN THESE HUGE "POOR MAN'S UMBRELLA" LEAVES REVEAL THE ACID'S STRENGTH. DURING ONE LIGHT RAIN THE ACID IRRITATED OUR EYES SO MUCH WE COULD BARELY SEE OUR WAY ALONG THE TRAIL. DESPITE OUR WEARING PROTECTIVE MASKS, THE INSIDES OF OUR MOUTHS BECAME BLISTERED, AND OUR VOICES AND BREATHING WERE AFFECTED FOR WEEKS.

LARGER THAN LIFE, THIS GAPING, 1.5-KILOMETER-WIDE CRATER (ONE OF FIVE) ON POÁS VOLCANO LOOKS LIKE A CHARRED AMPHITHEATER AND SMOLDERING STAGE. THE STEAM RISES FROM A SULFUR-STAINED VENT FILLED WITH A GREEN LAKE AND MUD THAT REACHES THE BOILING POINT. EVERY FEW MINUTES A MUTED JETTING SOUND ECHOES ACROSS THE CRATER. GEYSERS STRAINING THROUGH THE LAKE FORCE HOT WATER AND STEAM INTO A BILLOWING PLUME. IN 1989 POÁS EXPERIENCED AN ASH ERUPTION; SINCE THEN IT HAS BEEN HOT BUT INDECISIVE. (COSTA RICA)

A PARTY OF VOLCANO WATCHERS FOLLOWS AN ARC OF STEAM TO A SMOLDERING CLIFF. JUST OUT OF SIGHT, A RIVER OF LAVA SLIDES INTO THE SEA. (HAWAII)

RIPPED OPEN LIKE A CADAVER, WHITE ISLAND VOLCANO EXPOSES ITS TROUBLED INTERIOR. THICK BRAIDS OF STEAM UNCOIL ABOVE CONGRESS VENT. TO THE RIGHT ANOTHER SMALLER VENT, FILLED WITH MUD, BOILS IMPATIENTLY. OCCASIONALLY THE STEAM IS STAINED WITH ASH, REVEALING THAT GROUND WATER HAS TOUCHED RISING MAGMA. THE MAORI PEOPLE NAMED THE ISLAND *WHAKARI*, MEANING "SUSPENDED FROM HEAVEN BY A WHITE CLOUD." CAPTAIN COOK, THE FIRST EUROPEAN TO SEE THE VOLCANO, CALLED IT WHITE ISLAND AFTER HE WITNESSED AN ERUPTION THAT DUSTED THE STRATOVOLCANO WITH WHITE ASH. WE TOOK THIS PHOTOGRAPH JUST TWO MONTHS AFTER THE VOLCANO REAWAKENED IN FEBRUARY 1986. (BAY OF PLENTY, NEW ZEALAND)

ERUPTING

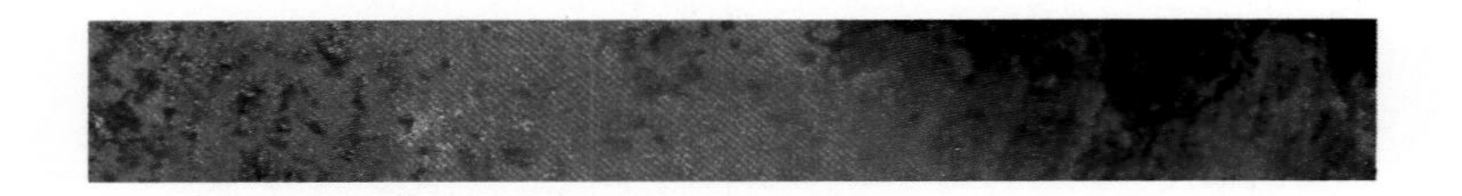

A flower erupts pollen,
A cloud erupts rain,
The evening sky erupts starlight,
The earth erupts.

ERUPTING

May 28, 1992. *Arenal has all the power and fury of a Hollywood-movie volcano. Its flawless, classic profile upstages the expansive, cobalt blue sky. It waits impatiently until we take our seats on a small observing platform about 2 kilometers away; then, as if on cue, it entertains us with hourly bursts of fire and ash until an intermission comes well past midnight.*

Standing black and massive against the starlit sky, Arenal sleeps until dawn. In seconds — before we have time to ready our cameras — a great, black cloud bolts out of the volcano and flies several kilometers into the sky! This is followed by a spray of incandescent lava bombs that slice through the ash cloud like lion claws into flesh. What a glorious and shocking sight to behold: the royal blue dawn, the silhouette of Arenal, the towering ash cloud, and the sky being ripped into bleeding shreds.

Six seconds pass before the blast hits. KABOOM! The shock wave shoves us, and we wonder if our last sight here on earth will be of this magnificent eruption. A volcanic meteor shower of glittering pink, orange, yellow, and red boulders — some the size of Volkswagens — fall out of the darkened cloud and smash like quicksilver onto the mountain's slopes. Liquid lightning opens into a golden fan as the rocks slide down the mountain with a terrible crunch like a thousand bones breaking. Then, without a bow, burning Arenal fades into the lavender curtain of twilight. The sun rises on another crystal blue morning in Costa Rica.

NOTHING ARENAL HAD DONE throughout the previous day and early evening prepared us for that fantastic dawn explosion. No matter how great or how many times a volcano blows in a day, there's always the chance its next eruption will be even more remarkable.

The world harbors many different types of volcanoes, and they all behave differently. Some, like Hawaii's volcanoes, erupt

---

A SINGED FINGER OF CLOUD LIFTS OFF BURNING ARENAL VOLCANO AS A VISCOUS BLOCK LAVA FLOW MARCHES DOWN THE MOUNTAIN'S SLOPES. BEFORE LEVELING OFF, THE FLOW SPLITS IN TWO THEN DIVIDES AGAIN. THIS ANDESITIC LAVA SMELLS LIKE BURNT, DUSTY METAL AND WHEN MOVING FORWARD SOUNDS LIKE WAGON WHEELS ROLLING OVER COBBLESTONES COVERED WITH BROKEN GLASS. (COSTA RICA)

quietly, overflowing with wide, sinuous lava rivers or immense fountains of fire; there are relatively few explosions. A Hawaiian-type eruption is as graceful to watch as a hula dancer. More explosive types, like Stromboli near Sicily, act like boxers throwing a series of punches; these staccato expulsions roar, hiss, and toss up sandwich-size bombs of blood red lava. The most powerful of all, the Plinian type, characterized by Mount Pinatubo in the Philippines, erupt with unfathomable energies that far surpass those contained in the world's entire arsenal of nuclear weapons.

Whether its style is fluid and slow or gaseous and powerful, a volcano erupts with a blind eye toward humanity. A lava flow isn't concerned with what lies in its path; it merely moves forward. Buildings, highways, and croplands have all been engulfed by lava. Efforts to stop lava flows by bombing them have had no discernible effect. Monstrous levies have been erected in their paths to little avail. As evidenced by places like Pompeii (which, after Italy's Mount Vesuvius erupted in A.D. 79, remained buried beneath 6 meters of volcanic ash for 2,000 years) and possibly legendary Atlantis (purportedly associated with the 1500 B.C. Santorini volcanic eruptions in the Aegean Sea, which buried the Minoan city of Akroteri), violent explosive events can erase entire civilizations in the geologic blink of an eye. We are powerless over volcanoes. Thousands of years after we have left this earth, volcanoes will live on.

BEFORE BEING CONSUMED BY FIRE, THIS STRANDED OHIA TREE CRIED OUT WITH A SHRILL WHISTLE. FLAMES LICK WILDLY AT ITS BRANCHES. LAVA FLOWING FROM KILAUEA VOLCANO STARTED THIS CRACKLING BRUSHFIRE, WHICH SWEPT THROUGH DOZENS OF ACRES OF DRY GRASS IN MINUTES. (HAWAII)

Celebrating life, Stromboli showers the night with lava sparklers. At other volcanoes around the world the sudden, explosive discharge of gas and lava, of the kind shown here, is known as Strombolian activity. (Lipari Islands, Italy)

AS FAITHFUL AS THE NORTH STAR, STROMBOLI SHOOTS OUT A LAVA BEACON ABOUT EVERY QUARTER HOUR. OVER THE CENTURIES STROMBOLI'S ERUPTIONS HAVE BECOME SO FAMILIAR TO SAILORS THAT THE VOLCANO IS KNOWN AS THE LIGHTHOUSE OF THE MEDITERRANEAN. (LIPARI ISLANDS, ITALY)

TRACER-BULLET STARS RAIN DOWN ON A BURNING VOLCANIC BATTLESHIP. ARENAL, A STRATOVOLCANO IN CENTRAL COSTA RICA, HAD ITS FIRST RECORDED ERUPTION ON JULY 29, 1968 — A VIOLENT EVENT THAT CLAIMED 80 LIVES AND DESTROYED 12 SQUARE KILOMETERS OF LAND. SINCE THEN THE VOLCANO HAS BEEN CONTINUOUSLY ACTIVE.

Through stone lips Hawaii's volcano goddess, Pele, drinks the golden nectar of Kupaianaha lava lake. This rare view shows the entrance to an active lava tube, which drains molten rock from the lake. The lava continues to flow underground in long tube systems until it spills out onto the coast or into the sea. Here, the lake drains forcefully, ripping apart the black surface crust and exposing its incandescent mantle. The broken pieces of crust float like rafts into the tube's throat, where they quickly dissolve.

To see a volcanic eruption is to witness the dawn of

Erupting

SINCE 1983 A CONTINUING ERUPTION OF KILAUEA VOLCANO — ITS LONGEST IN RECORDED HISTORY — HAS CLAIMED MORE THAN 180 HOMES AND OTHER STRUCTURES, BURIED SEVERAL KILOMETERS OF HIGHWAY, AND DESTROYED MANY ANCIENT HAWAIIAN TEMPLES AND NATURAL ATTRACTIONS.

THIS YELLOW ROAD OF LAVA LEADS TO THE LUSH, EMERALD SLOPES OF KILAUEA VOLCANO, WHERE IT OVERTAKES KALAPANA, HAWAII'S COLORFUL SEASIDE PARADISE.

MOLTEN SPATTER FLIES OUT OF PU 'U 'O 'O VENT ON KILAUEA VOLCANO. (HAWAII)

BEHOLD THE EYE OF A GODDESS. THIS AERIAL VIEW OF A SKYLIGHT IN THE CEILING OF A LAVA TUBE REVEALS A MOLTEN RIVER FLOWING BENEATH THE SURFACE OF KILAUEA VOLCANO. THE LAVA'S TEMPERATURE INSIDE THE TUBE IS MORE THAN 1,000°C. (HAWAII)

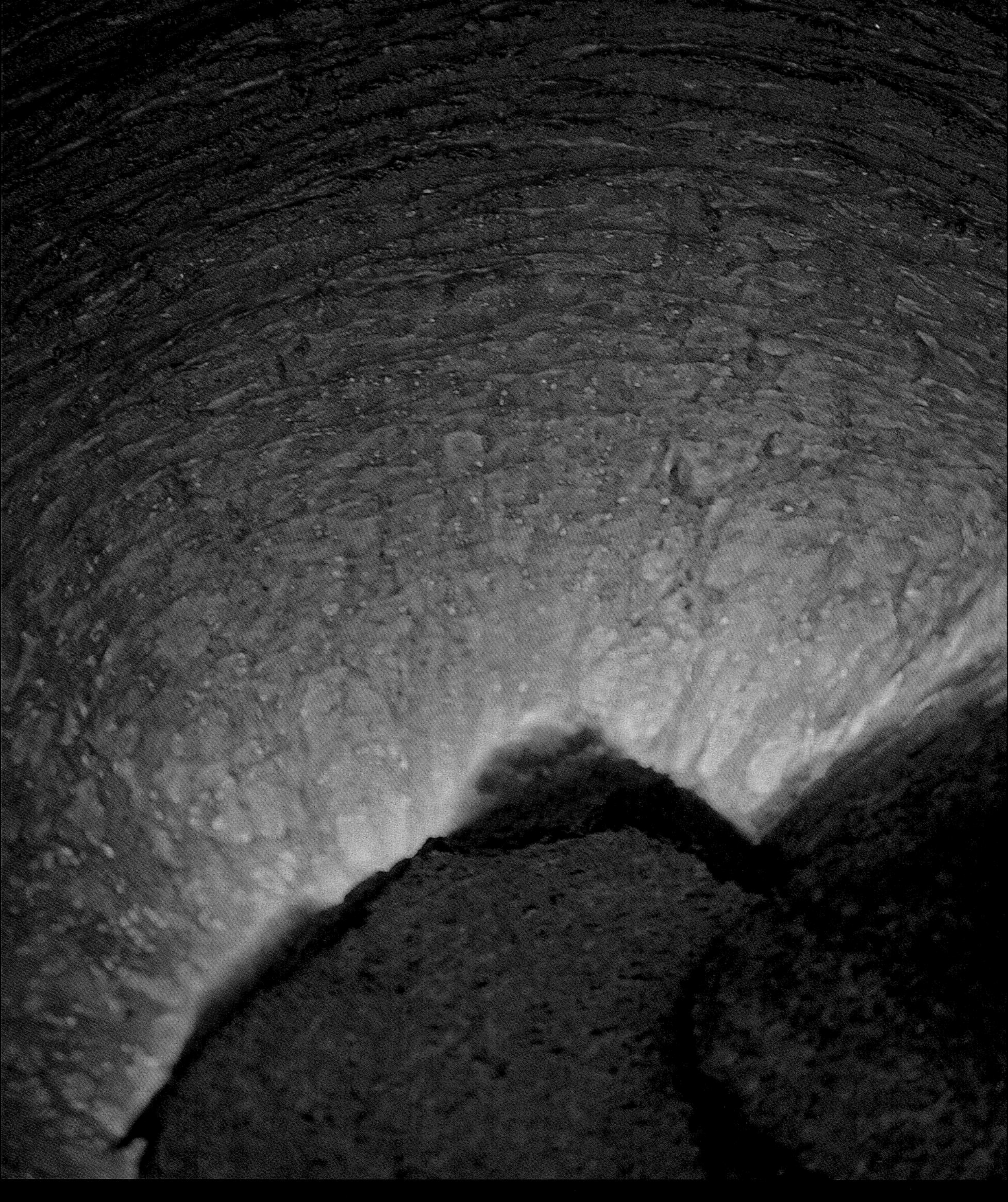

Ropy pahoehoe lava fans out in a vibrant palette of color. The lava streams forward sounding like Rice Krispies in milk, but it reeks of a smoky, metallic odor like burning sulfur wrapped in tarnished silver. (Hawaii)

A storm of wind which appeared to be cast forth from an immense ventilator roused up the interior fires of the earth. It was a hot, incandescent blast.

—Jules Verne, *A Journey to the Center of the Earth*

LIKE A BARGE OUT OF CONTROL, GUATEMALA CITY APPEARS TO BE SAILING DANGEROUSLY CLOSE TO A MIGHTY SPINE OF ACTIVE VOLCANOES. THE MOST PROMINENT CONE HERE IS 3,766-METER-HIGH AGUA VOLCANO. (GUATEMALA)

IN 1902 SANTA MARIA VOLCANO IN GUATEMALA ERUPTED CATASTROPHICALLY, KILLING 6,000 PEOPLE. TIME HAS PUT A BANDAGE OVER THE WOUND, HOWEVER, AND TODAY THE MOUNTAIN RISES IMPOSINGLY OVER QUETZALTENANGO, GUATEMALA'S SECOND MOST POPULOUS CITY. THE VOLCANO IS EXPECTED TO ERUPT DISASTROUSLY ONCE AGAIN BY THE END OF THE DECADE.

THE CYCLE OF LIFE IN HAWAII IS WELL KNOWN. THE ISLANDS ARE BORN OF FIRE AND GROW TO GREAT PROMINENCE. ONCE THE ERUPTIONS STOP, THE NUTRIENT-RICH LAVAS TRIGGER RAPID PLANT GROWTH, WHICH CAN EVOLVE INTO LUSH TROPICAL RAIN FORESTS *(OPPOSITE PAGE)*.

Sleeping

AS THE HAWAIIAN ISLANDS AGE, THEY ARE ERODED BY THE ACTIONS OF WIND, RAIN, AND SURF *(OPPOSITE AND ABOVE)*. THE ISLANDS SLOWLY RECEDE INTO THE SEA. OVER THE MILLENNIA THE ISLANDS ARE ERASED BY WATER AND WIND.

As seen from the summit of Mount Vesuvius, the sun-bleached houses surrounding Naples look like flakes of dandruff brushed off the mountain's swollen shoulders. Since March 1944 the volcano has been suspiciously quiet. A major eruption now seems imminent, a fact that wears heavily on the minds of Neapolitans who still live near the volcano's slopes. (Italy)

Dawn breaks over Mount Vesuvius, the most famous of all volcanoes. The A.D. 79 eruption that annihilated Pompeii and Herculaneum was not actually of Vesuvius but of Monte Somma; Vesuvius grew out of the remains of that ancient volcano, though the two names are used synonymously today. Here, the curved ridge of Monte Somma can be seen to the left of symmetrical Vesuvius. (Italy)

Volcanic peril does not wait for man. . . . Human history is full of stories echoing with the cry of buried towns. . . . Such catastrophes are explained by the snare that lies for swarming humanity in the exceptional fertility of volcanic regions.

—Haroun Tazieff, *Craters of Fire*

Volcanoes Highlighted in this Book

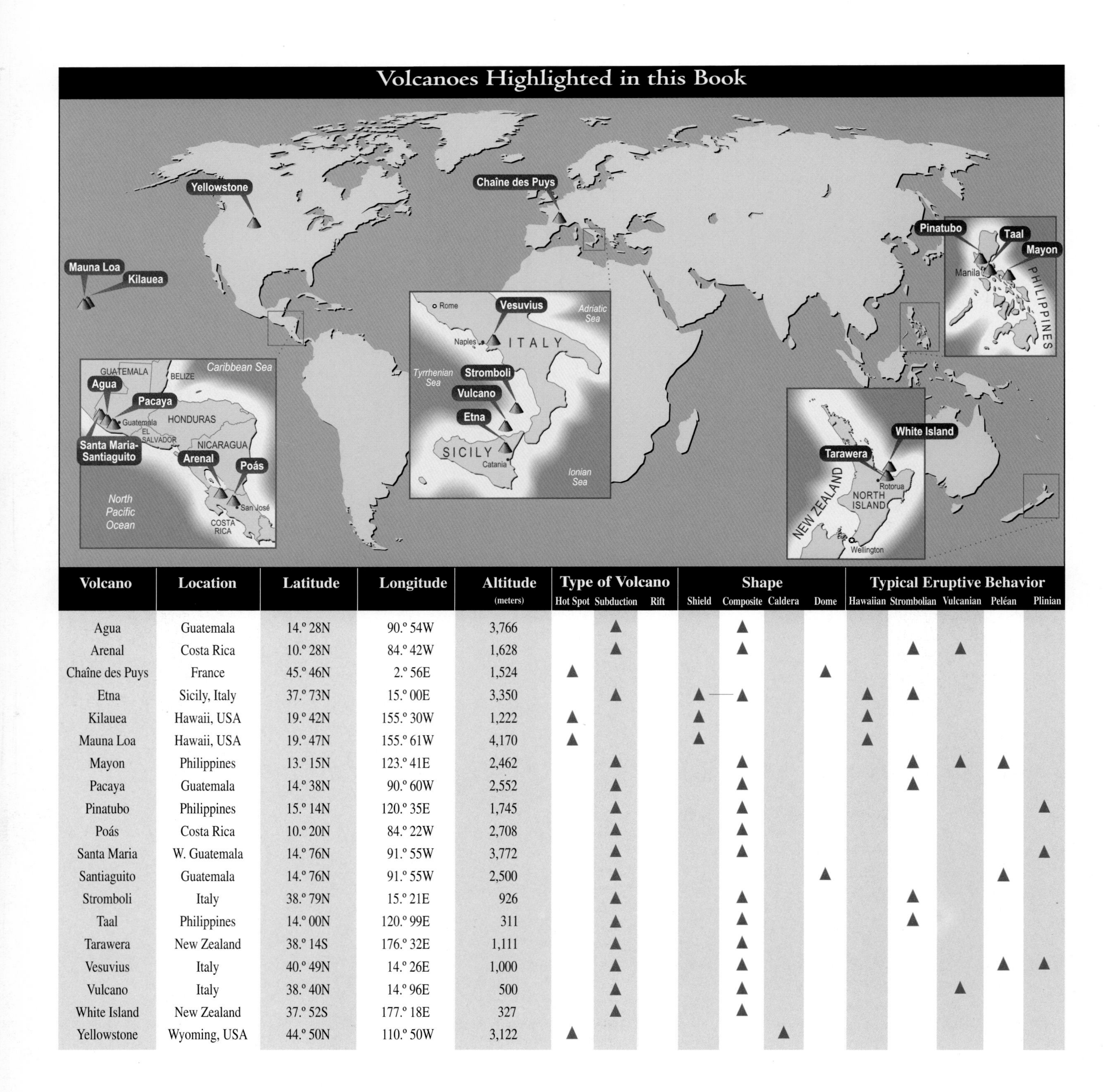

Volcano	Location	Latitude	Longitude	Altitude (meters)	Type of Volcano			Shape				Typical Eruptive Behavior				
					Hot Spot	Subduction	Rift	Shield	Composite	Caldera	Dome	Hawaiian	Strombolian	Vulcanian	Peléan	Plinian
Agua	Guatemala	14.° 28N	90.° 54W	3,766		▲			▲							
Arenal	Costa Rica	10.° 28N	84.° 42W	1,628		▲			▲				▲	▲		
Chaîne des Puys	France	45.° 46N	2.° 56E	1,524	▲						▲					
Etna	Sicily, Italy	37.° 73N	15.° 00E	3,350		▲		▲ —	▲			▲	▲			
Kilauea	Hawaii, USA	19.° 42N	155.° 30W	1,222	▲			▲				▲				
Mauna Loa	Hawaii, USA	19.° 47N	155.° 61W	4,170	▲			▲				▲				
Mayon	Philippines	13.° 15N	123.° 41E	2,462		▲			▲				▲	▲	▲	
Pacaya	Guatemala	14.° 38N	90.° 60W	2,552		▲			▲				▲			
Pinatubo	Philippines	15.° 14N	120.° 35E	1,745		▲			▲							▲
Poás	Costa Rica	10.° 20N	84.° 22W	2,708		▲			▲							
Santa Maria	W. Guatemala	14.° 76N	91.° 55W	3,772		▲			▲							▲
Santiaguito	Guatemala	14.° 76N	91.° 55W	2,500		▲					▲				▲	
Stromboli	Italy	38.° 79N	15.° 21E	926		▲			▲				▲			
Taal	Philippines	14.° 00N	120.° 99E	311		▲			▲				▲			
Tarawera	New Zealand	38.° 14S	176.° 32E	1,111		▲			▲							
Vesuvius	Italy	40.° 49N	14.° 26E	1,000		▲			▲						▲	▲
Vulcano	Italy	38.° 40N	14.° 96E	500		▲			▲					▲		
White Island	New Zealand	37.° 52S	177.° 18E	327		▲			▲							
Yellowstone	Wyoming, USA	44.° 50N	110.° 50W	3,122	▲					▲						

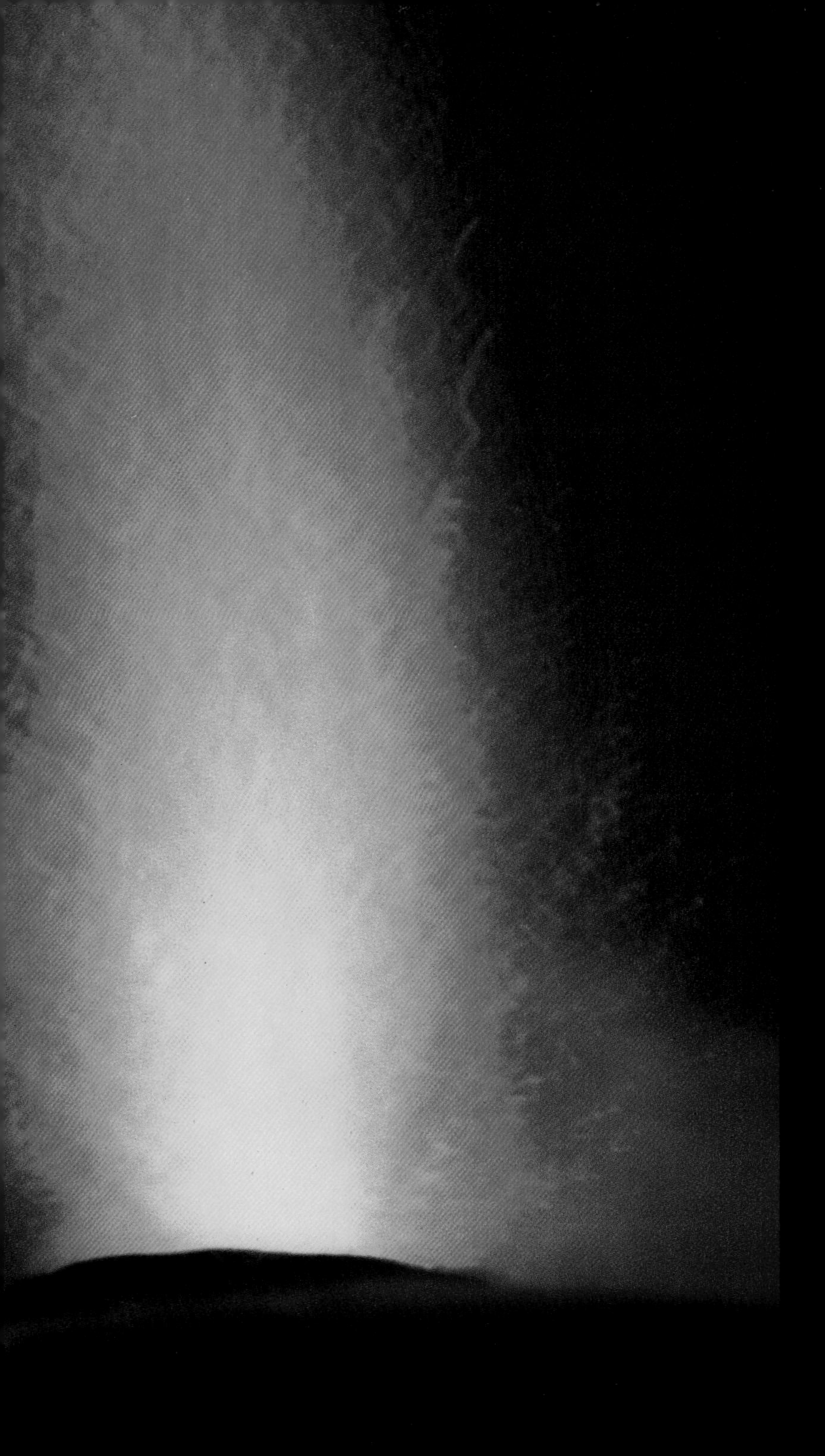

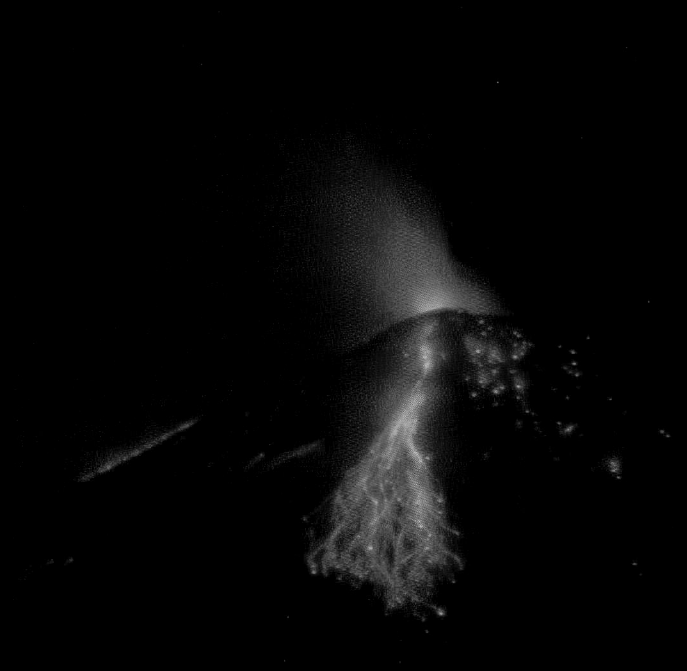

A firestorm of lava and ash ignites the sky over Arenal volcano in Costa Rica. Incandescent boulders ejected from the crater trace erratic paths as they race downslope.

A tornado of fire screams out of Stromboli volcano. Triggered by a mighty gas explosion, the blast sends a myriad of lava blocks whirling on corkscrew paths through the blue-velvet dusk. Descriptions of such awesome activity inspired Jules Verne to end his *Journey to the Center of the Earth* with Harry, Gretchen, and Professor Hardwigg being tossed out of Stromboli in "a wild whirlwind of flame." (Lipari Islands, Italy)

A black mountain grows within a black mountain. In 1963 Pacaya volcano exploded to life, quickly forming a large cinder cone (MacKenney cone) within an ancient horseshoe-shaped caldera. Here, in November 1992, it displays weak Strombolian activity, spewing small clouds of cinder several hundred times a day. Smoke also rises from three dark andesitic lava flows creeping down the cone's northern slope. Only 32 kilometers from Guatemala City, Pacaya is a popular tourist attraction. It was once proposed that a hotel be built at the volcano's base, an idea no longer welcomed.

In an area the size of New York City's Central Park a fissure rips open on a slope of Mauna Loa volcano and shoots out a wall of fire. For nearly three weeks the volcano has been pumping out some 440,000 cubic meters of lava per hour! The lava spills out of its stone kettle and feeds a 6-meter-wide lava river that stretches 26 kilometers from the active vent. The eruption, which began on March 25, 1984, and ended 21 days later, contributed 220 million cubic meters of new land to the island — enough lava to pave a 5-meter-wide, 1-meter-thick highway that could encircle the globe. (Hawaii)

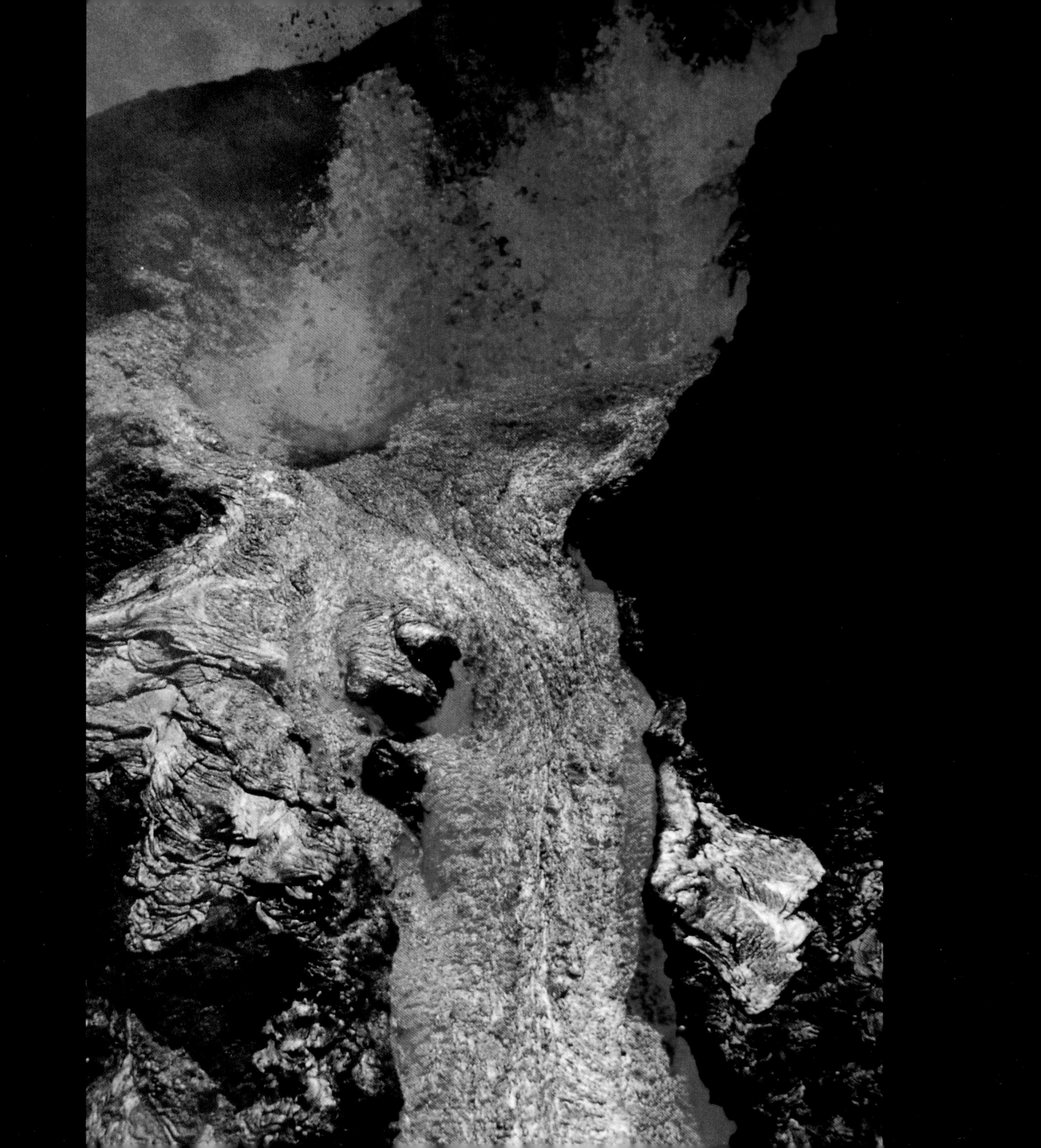

WITH A DEAFENING ROAR THE CEILING OF A 10-METER-WIDE LAVA TUBE COLLAPSES INTO AN ORANGE TORRENT OF MOLTEN ROCK. WHAT WAS ONCE SOLID EARTH IS NOW A SEARING GASH IN A JAGGED, BLACK CLIFF. AS IF STUNNED BY THE FALL, TWO COLOSSAL LAVA BLOCKS SIT DUMBFOUNDED ON A SLAG-COVERED SHORELINE. (HAWAII)

A GROUP OF DARING TOURISTS GETS TERRIBLY CLOSE TO AN ORANGE RIBBON OF LAVA THREADING ITS WAY TO THE SEA. (HAWAII)

AFTER HAVING BEEN SPIT OUT OF THE EARTH AND BLOWN OUT OF THE SEA, A FLYING SQUADRON OF STEAMING BLACK LAVA BLOCKS LANDS SOFTLY — AND IN FORMATION — ON A NEWLY FORMED BLACK-SAND BEACH. (HAWAII)

EACH YEAR MILLIONS OF VISITORS FLOCK TO KILAUEA VOLCANO IN HAWAII VOLCANOES NATIONAL PARK, MANY HOPING TO WITNESS A SPECTACULAR LAVA SHOW. FOR THE LAST DECADE AND MORE, KILAUEA HAS LET FEW OF THEM DOWN.

LIKE DANTE SEEING THE "FLAMING RED TOWERS OF DIS, THE CAPITAL OF HELL," WE ARE GREETED WITH DUAL BLASTS FROM STROMBOLI VOLCANO. THE FIRES FRAME A PORTHOLE TO THE SEETHING UNDERWORLD, WHICH CAN BE SEEN ONLY BY THOSE WHO VENTURE TO THE MOUNTAIN'S SUMMIT. (LIPARI ISLANDS, ITALY)

we came
to the foot of a Great Tower; but long before
we reached it through the marsh, two horns of flame

flared from the summit, one from either side.

—Dante, *The Inferno*

THE "BLACK PEARL WITH A HEART OF FIRE," STROMBOLI VOLCANO THROWS OUT CLOTS OF LAVA THAT DANCE WILDLY IN THE WIND. THE ERUPTION BEGINS WITH A JET-ENGINE SOUND THAT BUILDS TO A ROAR AS GASES WITHIN THE MOUNTAIN SHOOT THROUGH LAVA COLLECTING IN ITS VENTS. (LIPARI ISLANDS, ITALY)

A FIST OF ASH PUNCHES THE SKY ABOVE ARENAL VOLCANO IN COSTA RICA. THE BLOW RATTLES THE WINDOWS AT A LOOKOUT 2.7 KILOMETERS AWAY. THE ACCOMPANYING ***ROAR*** FRIGHTENS VISITORS FROM THEIR SEATS. BOULDERS THE SIZE OF TV SETS SMASH ONTO THE MOUNTAIN'S SUMMIT. SOME DISINTEGRATE IN A PUFF OF GRAY SMOKE, WHILE OTHERS TUMBLE AND CHATTER DOWNSLOPE. POWERFUL VULCANIAN ERUPTIONS, LIKE THE ONE SHOWN HERE, ARE A PART OF MANY TYPICAL PATTERNS OF ACTIVITY AT ARENAL. THIS EVENT WAS ONE OF 34 SIMILAR ONES RECORDED DURING A 24-HOUR VIGIL THAT BEGAN AT 8 A.M. ON MAY 27, 1992.

Grumbling as it awakens, Arenal clears its throat of ash. A churning gray cloud rises from the mountain, then nudges a passing cumulus cloud before the volcano returns to sleep; the mountain will erupt again in about an hour. (Costa Rica)

Pelted by volcanic stones and ash, a wounded tree kneels before mighty Mount Pinatubo in the Philippines. A few leaves manage to cling to gnarled branches. On April 2, 1991, Mount Pinatubo awakened for the first time in recorded history. That June it erupted continuously for 15 hours, throwing ash 40 kilometers into the atmosphere and sandblasting villages surrounding the volcano. Ash fell like snow in Manila, 100 kilometers to its south. (Luzon Island)

see in the wall
a stone archway, and out of the barrow broke
a stream surging through it, a stream of fire
with waves of deadly flame; the dragon's breath
. . . billowed from the rock
in a hissing gust; the ground boomed.

—*Beowulf*

PULSING, THROBBING, AND SPLASHING, THE LIFEBLOOD OF MAUNA LOA VOLCANO GUSHES OUT OF A WOUND IN THE VOLCANO'S NECK. (HAWAII)

HIGH ON AN ICE-DAPPLED WALL IN MOUNT ETNA'S VALLE DEL BOVE, A SPRING OF MOLTEN LAVA LEAKS FROM A LONG FISSURE. THE GROUND TREMBLES REPEATEDLY AS SMOKE AND FIRE BLOW OUT OF HOLES IN THE ROCK. BETWEEN BLASTS SPINE-CHILLING SOUNDS OF BREATHING ISSUE FROM THE CRACK AND ECHO OFF THE VALLEY WALLS. HOW EASY IT WOULD HAVE BEEN FOR OUR ANCESTORS TO BELIEVE IN FIRE-BREATHING DRAGONS. (SICILY)

SLUGGISH IN MANNER, A 5-METER-THICK FLOW OF AA LAVA HEAVES FORWARD, AS IF IT'S BEING PUSHED BY A BULLDOZER. COOLING LAVA BLOCKS ROLL DOWN THE FLOW'S INCANDESCENT FACE AND SHATTER LIKE GLASS. AA LAVA IS MORE VISCOUS AND FRAGMENTARY THAN PAHOEHOE LAVA (FOREGROUND) BECAUSE IT HAS LOST ALMOST ALL OF ITS GAS. (HAWAII)

PAHOEHOE LAVA CAN FORM A THIN, BRITTLE SHELL. THIS BASALTIC ROCK, ENCASED IN FLUID GLASS, POURS OUT SMOOTHLY THEN WRINKLES WHEN IT HITS OLDER ROCK. (HAWAII)

Color is a good indicator of a lava flow's temperature and viscosity: the brighter the color, the more fluid the flow. Red lava is between 815° and 1,040°C; orange, between 1,040° and 1,150°C; and yellow, between 1,150° and 1,260°C. (Hawaii)

Furious steam clouds hammer at the sky above Kamoamoa, Hawaii. As if oblivious to the turmoil, two visitors stop to admire the region's undulating ocean of black rock.

Earth, water, wind, and fire battle in the Puna district of Hawaii.

Puna is shaking in the wind,
Shaking is the hala grove of Keaau.
Tumbling are Haena and Hopoe,
Moving is the land — moving is the sea.

—W. D. Westervelt, *Myths and Legends of Hawaii*

Stromboli, Italy's stone leviathan, spurts liquid fire from a burning blowhole. A single volcanic construct with a surface area of 12.6 square kilometers, Stromboli rises a mere 924 meters above sea level. Measured from the sea floor, however, it's some 3,200 meters high — second only to Mount Etna as the tallest mountain in Italy.

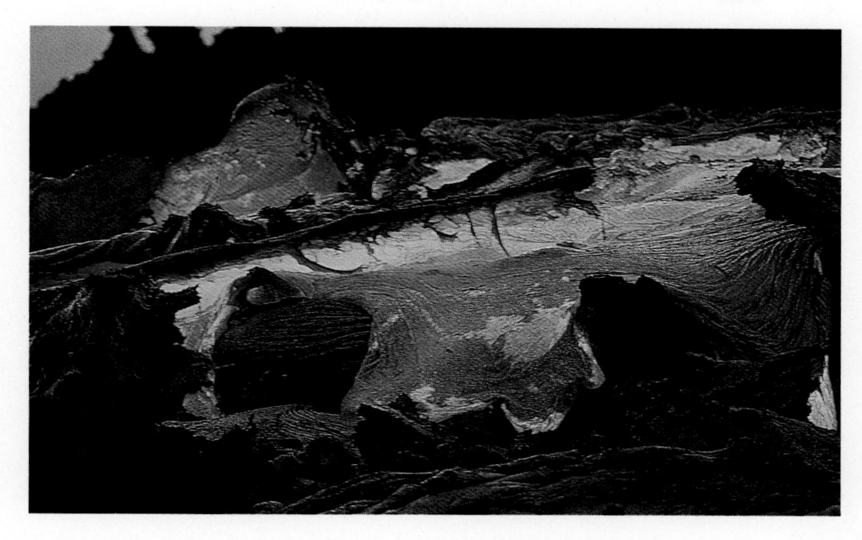

PAHOEHOE LAVA STRAYS FROM ITS PARENT FLOW AND PLOWS INTO A CUL-DE-SAC OF TWISTED RUBBLE. ITS OLDER, BLACK CRUST BREAKS APART IN THE COLLISION AND IS CONSUMED BY A MOLTEN INTERIOR. THE DOOMED FLOW WILL SPREAD OUT, LOSE GAS AND HEAT, AND SOLIDIFY. (HAWAII)

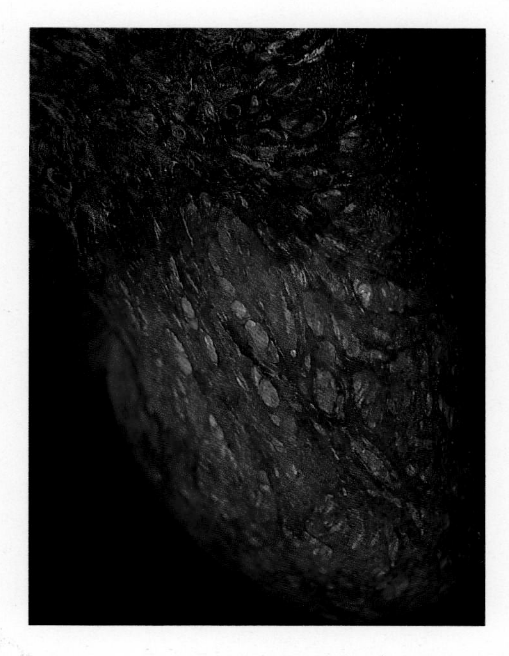

AS IF TAKING A DEEP BREATH, A STONE LUNG EXPANDS. LAVA'S COOLING SKIN CAN STRETCH WHEN ITS MOLTEN INTERIOR INFLATES. (HAWAII)

SANTIAGUITO DOME SPOUTS A THICK COLUMN OF ASH. IT IS ONE OF FOUR ERUPTIONS THAT OCCURRED ABOUT EVERY HOUR DURING OUR NOVEMBER 1992 VISIT. THE TWO LIGHT GRAY TRACKS OF DEBRIS ON THE DOME ARE ACTUALLY A BLOCK LAVA FLOW AND A PYROCLASTIC-FLOW CHANNEL. SANTIAGUITO POSES AN IMMEDIATE THREAT TO FARMERS WHO WORK THE FIELDS NEARBY (FOREGROUND) BECAUSE IT IS BULGING AND MIGHT HAVE A LATERAL EXPLOSION — LIKE MOUNT ST. HELENS DID IN 1980. (GUATEMALA)

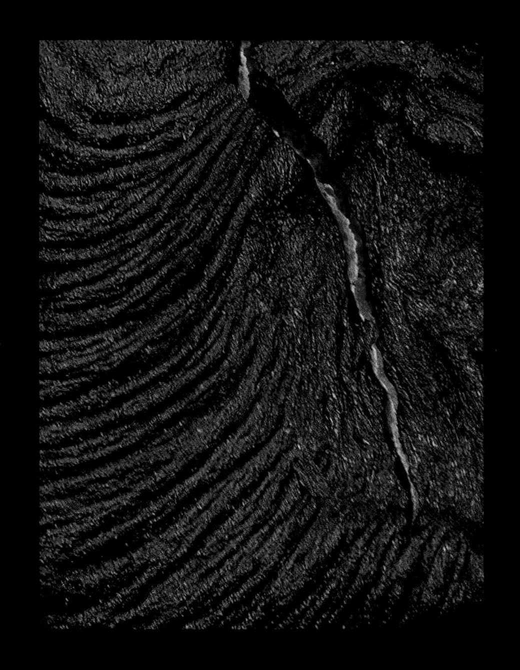

When the heavens shake,
When the earth cracks open,
Man is thrown down,
Lying on the ground.
The lightning of Kane (a great god) wakes up.

. . . .

E ala e! Wake up!

—W. D. Westervelt, *Myths and Legends of Hawaii*

ABOVE: CAPTURED IN A RARE MOMENT, A GREAT, TURBULENT CLOUD OF STEAM, FORMED BY LAVA SURGING INTO THE SEA, IS PUSHED ON ITS SIDE BY STRONG WINDS. THE CLOUD'S BASE ROLLS INTO A PENDULOUS, SWIRLING FUNNEL CLOUD. *BELOW:* THE CLIFF-SIDE END OF THE FUNNEL BREAKS FREE AND TOUCHES DOWN ON THE SEA'S SURFACE AS A WATERSPOUT. (HAWAII)

FIERY SERPENTS OF LAVA SLITHER INTO THE SEA. THE OCEAN HISSES IN DISGUST AND FLEES TO THE SKY AS STEAM. (HAWAII)

IN UTTER SILENCE A HIDEOUS FIGUREHEAD OF ASH CHARGES DOWN THE SLOPES OF MOUNT MAYON IN THE PHILIPPINES; SEARING-HOT PARTICLES FALL OUT OF THE CLOUD, PERILOUSLY CLOSE TO A SLEEPING VILLAGE. THE DEADLIEST OF ALL VOLCANIC HAZARDS, PYROCLASTIC FLOWS, ALSO CALLED *NUÉE ARDENTE* (FRENCH FOR GLOWING AVALANCHE), TRAVEL WITH SPEEDS OF MORE THAN 100 KILOMETERS PER HOUR AND INCINERATE EVERYTHING IN THEIR PATHS. THEY FORM FROM EITHER THE COLLAPSE OF A HEAVY ASH COLUMN OR THE DISINTEGRATION OF A LAVA DOME, WHICH IS THE CASE HERE. SUCH ACTIVITY IS TYPICAL OF A PELÉAN-TYPE ERUPTION, NAMED FOR THE 1902 ERUPTION OF MOUNT PELÉE, WHOSE NUÉE ARDENTE KILLED 28,000 PEOPLE IN THE CARIBBEAN TOWN OF ST. PIERRE ON MARTINIQUE. (LUZON ISLAND)

DRAPED IN OLDER GLOBS OF MELDED SILVER, A WINDOW OPENS ON A PAHOEHOE LAVA FLOW AND REVEALS ITS LIQUID SOUL. A SUSTAINED PAHOEHOE FLOW CAN FORM AN INSULATING CEILING THAT ALLOWS ITS MOLTEN INTERIOR TO TRAVEL GREAT DISTANCES AT EXTREMELY HIGH TEMPERATURES. (HAWAII)

Chained by sunbeams, a defenseless palm tree awaits inevitable death by fire. The lava has already flowed several kilometers down Kilauea volcano and devoured Kalapana, a colorful village on the Big Island of Hawaii. Now it looks determined to push forward, and not even the sea will alter its course.

A mock sun rises as liquid rock burns through a cliff on Hawaii's Kilauea.

In the strong light every countenance glowed like red-hot iron. . . . The place below looked like the infernal regions and these men like half-cooled devils just come up on a furlough.

—Mark Twain, *Mark Twain's Letters from Hawaii*

Sleeping

A child sleeps,
Trees in winter sleep,
Coral cups sleep under the sea,
Among the mountains, a volcano sleeps.

SLEEPING

February 25, 1990. *A narrow stream of lava breaks out of the earth on Kilauea volcano. Its tangerine-colored skin is freckled with gray and undulates as the fluid rock rolls forward. The crack where the lava emerges seals up quickly, severing the stream's umbilical-like connection to the earth's interior. Without nourishment the lava flow cannot last long. It slows, meanders a bit, tumbles over a tiny hill, then flops down onto level ground.*

There the lava collects and chatters — a cacophony of crunching, cackling, and popping — like thousands of high-pitched voices disagreeing over what to do next. No matter, the flow is doomed. In its final moments the pool swells, conforming to the contour of the surrounding rocks. On the slope of Kilauea volcano that flow has made its final bed. A silver chrysalis of silken stone slowly forms on the skin of the lava flow. Wrapped in this insulating blanket, the lava falls asleep.

WHEN A FLUID VOLCANO stops erupting it is like an ocean turning to stone. Lava, swaying to a fiery rhythm of life, becomes a dark and somber landscape, its motion suddenly frozen in time. When it cools and hardens a lava flow exhibits the volcano's artistry on a rippled canvas of rock. Each frozen current tells a story: how it was born, where it originated, and where it was heading. Kilauea volcano in Hawaii is a monument to such masterpieces. It is an ever-evolving canvas because Kilauea is still in the process of growing.

Once a Hawaiian flow is stilled, and the air currents above the mountains stir, the winds transport a valuable cargo: tiny seeds, fragile pioneers in a stone desert, which will be the first life to colonize the sleeping lava in a few short months. As winds and weather abrade the hardened flow, coarse soil forms, providing a place for seedlings to take hold and develop roots. A brand-new forest begins. The wind also carries insects and spiders holding

---

LIKE SPILLED PUDDING, THIS PAHOEHOE FLOW (A TYPE CALLED ENTRAIL LAVA) OOZES ACROSS THE SOUTHEAST SLOPE OF KILAUEA VOLCANO, ADDING HEIGHT TO THE MOUNTAIN. GENTLY SLOPING SHIELD VOLCANOES, LIKE KILAUEA, GROW BY THE ACCUMULATION OF THOUSANDS OF SUCH FLUID OUTPOURINGS FROM THE VOLCANO'S SUMMIT AND SLOPES. (HAWAII)

their silken threads aloft like parachuters ready to tumble upon the new vegetation and soil. Birds, bats, and other small creatures find the insects and seeds. They help to disperse the seeds and pollinate the region, strengthening the forest's hold. One day a new forest will stand where an old forest may once have stood. People may populate the region out of necessity to farm the fertile soil. Villages and cities may grow up as people construct hotels, condominiums, skyscrapers, and geothermal plants — all for the benefit of humanity. With time people will forget the region's history until one day when the mountain reasserts itself and the cycle of life and death continues.

What is born of fire dies of fire, and there is little we can do to intervene. In this way it seems the planet itself keeps things in balance.

At home it's easy to get caught up in the chaos of city life. That's when we take a moment to remember our friends, the volcanoes we have known. Volcanoes offer perspective in a human culture that seeks to obscure or repress the natural cycle of death in life. They give us a better outlook on the meaning of our own lives. Volcanoes have taught us to take the time to live, richly and fully. We thank them for sparing us their fury and for bringing passion into our lives. We hope that, after we are gone, volcanoes will awaken this passion in others.

ONCE THE SITE OF TOWERING LAVA FOUNTAINS, THIS GLOWING VENT ON PU'U 'O'O CINDER CONE IN HAWAII HAS STOPPED ERUPTING. NOW ONLY A SMOKING CHIMNEY, THE VENT ALLOWS GASES TO ESCAPE FROM THE MOLTEN ROCK THAT STILL FLOWS BENEATH IT.

Of thundering Aetna, whose combustible
And fuell'd entrails thence conceiving fire,
Sublim'd with mineral fury, aid the winds,
And leave a singed bottom all involv'd
With stench and smoke.

—Milton, *Paradise Lost*

THE SKIN OF COOLED PAHOEHOE LAVA CAN BE EITHER SMOOTH OR RIPPLED LIKE FOLDED VELVET. (HAWAII)

AFTER 473 DAYS OF CONTINUOUS LAVA FLOWS MOUNT ETNA STOPS ERUPTING ON MARCH 30, 1993. THREE WEEKS LATER, HOWEVER, THE COLOSSUS CONTINUES TO BREATHE. HERE, A JET OF STEAM RISES ABOVE THE VOLCANO'S ICE-STREAKED SUMMIT, WHERE ANGRY WINDS PUSH THE CONDENSING BREATH ASIDE. (SICILY)

IT COULD HAPPEN TODAY OR 20 YEARS FROM NOW, BUT VULCANO IN THE LIPARI ISLANDS WILL ERUPT AGAIN — A PERILOUS SITUATION FOR THE HUNDREDS OF SICILIANS LIVING ON THE ISLAND. CALLED THE ANCESTOR OF ALL VOLCANOES, VULCANO LAST ERUPTED IN 1888. THE WORD *VOLCANO* COMES FROM VULCANO, THE ROMAN GOD OF FIRE WHOSE MYTHIC FORGE WAS HERE. (ITALY)

TODAY VULCANO FUMES CONTINUOUSLY AND OMINOUSLY. VISITORS TO THE ISLAND ARE IMMEDIATELY GREETED WITH THE ODOR OF ROTTEN EGGS FROM HYDROGEN-SULFIDE GAS.

Sleeping

THESE INNOCENTLY ROLLING MOUNDS COMPOSE THE NORTHERN TIP OF THE CHAÎNE DES PUYS IN CENTRAL FRANCE. ALTHOUGH THEY ARE ANCIENT DOMES OF VISCOUS LAVA THAT ERUPTED THOUSANDS OF YEARS AGO, THE REGION REMAINS VOLCANICALLY ACTIVE AND COULD CONCEIVABLY ERUPT AGAIN.

DARK AND GLOOMY, MOUNT TARAWERA IS THE SITE OF NEW ZEALAND'S GREATEST RECORDED VOLCANIC EVENT. ON JUNE 10, 1886, THE MOUNTAIN LITERALLY RIPPED OPEN AND HURLED OUT LAVA AND ASH FROM A STRING OF 20 CRATERS. PRIOR TO THE ERUPTION SEVERAL EUROPEANS HAD SEEN A PHANTOM MAORI WAR CANOE SAILING ON LAKE TARAWERA (SEEN HERE IN THE DISTANCE). WHEN ASKED ABOUT THE APPARITION A MAORI CHIEF SAID, "IT IS AN OMEN; IT IS A SIGN AND A WARNING THAT ALL THIS REGION WILL BE OVERWHELMED." (NORTH ISLAND)

SERENITY CONCEALS CATASTROPHE AT TAAL VOLCANO IN THE PHILIPPINES. A LUSH AND FERTILE VOLCANIC ISLAND NEAR THE CENTER OF TAAL LAKE — ITSELF A PREHISTORIC CALDERA ONLY 60 KILOMETERS SOUTH OF MANILA — TAAL VOLCANO IS A NOTORIOUS KILLER. ON JANUARY 30, 1911, IT ERUPTED EXPLOSIVELY, SPREADING ASH AND MUD ACROSS 2,000 SQUARE KILOMETERS AND EXTINGUISHING 1,335 LIVES. ANOTHER ERUPTION IN 1965 CLAIMED 190 LIVES. SEVERAL TIMES SINCE, TAAL HAS DISPLAYED LESS VIOLENT ACTIVITY. IN 1991 THE ISLAND WAS EVACUATED WHEN THE VOLCANO BEGAN TO TREMBLE. IT DID NOT ERUPT; HOWEVER, IT IS ONLY A MATTER OF TIME BEFORE IT DOES AGAIN. A MERE 311 METERS HIGH, TAAL IS AMONG THE WORLD'S LOWEST VOLCANOES. (LUZON ISLAND)

GLOSSARY

aa (AH-ah) The Hawaiian term for a chunky, sluggish, basaltic lava flow with a thick, incandescent interior and a dark, jumbled, jagged surface.

andesite A gray volcanic rock with a *silica* content between *basalt* and *dacite*. When molten, its *viscosity* is moderate to high.

ash Dust-size volcanic particles created during an explosive eruption.

basalt A black volcanic rock containing less than 53 percent *silica*. When molten, its *viscosity* is low.

block lava A type of lava flow common to andesitic volcanoes (such as Arenal in Costa Rica) that is thicker and moves more slowly than basaltic *aa*.

bomb A large lava fragment ejected during an eruption, commonly football-shaped or disk-shaped if flattened by impact.

caldera A great oval or circular depression (measuring 1½ kilometers or more in diameter) at the summit of a volcano.

cinder Fine volcanic ejecta measuring about 1 centimeter in diameter.

composite volcano A steep-sided volcano composed of different layers of lava flows, ejected fragments, and *pyroclastic flows*. Mount Mayon in the Philippines and Mount Vesuvius in Italy are examples. Also called a *stratovolcano*.

cone A steep hill of cinder, spatter, and other volcanic fragments surrounding a *vent*.

crater A bowl- or funnel-shaped depression (smaller than a *caldera*) at the mouth of a volcano.

dacite A light-colored volcanic rock with a silica content (63–68 percent) between *rhyolite* and *andesite*. When molten, it is highly viscous.

dome A steep-sided mound of viscous lava that gradually rises out of a volcanic vent after an explosive eruption.

entrail lava A type of *pahoehoe* lava named for its appearance.

fissure A rip or fracture on the surface of a volcano through which molten lava occasionally erupts.

fumarole A vent that emits volcanic gases and water vapor.

geyser A hot spring that periodically ejects columns of water and steam into the air. The word is derived from *geysa* (Icelandic, to gush).

Hawaiian-type eruption Characterized by nonexplosive outpourings of fluid lava that build a gently sloping shield volcano.

hornito A steep-sided volcanic *cone* several meters high formed by welded *spatter*.

hot spot A relatively fixed area of unusually hot rock in the upper *mantle*, just below the crust.

hot-spot volcano A volcano that forms over a hot spot. Hawaii's volcanoes are good examples.

lava Molten rock extruded from a volcanic vent and onto the earth's surface, where it solidifies; lava beneath the earth's crust is called *magma*.

lava lake Lava that has pooled over a volcanic vent or flowed into and filled a depression.

lava tube A subterranean tunnel that forms when the surface of a lava flow crusts over while it is still flowing. When the eruption stops, the lava drains, leaving behind a hollow tube.

magma Molten rock beneath the earth's crust; molten rock that flows onto the earth's surface is called *lava*.

magma chamber An underground reservoir of magma that fuels volcanic eruptions.

mantle The region of earth below the crust and above the core. Convection currents within the upper mantle may be partly responsible for the motion of crustal plates (see *plate tectonics*).

nuée ardente See *pyroclastic flow*.

pahoehoe (puh-HOY-hoy) A Hawaiian term for the fluid lava that solidifies with a smooth or ropy surface.

Peléan-type eruption Characterized by the fast-moving avalanches of hot ash and debris that travel down a volcano's slopes (see *pyroclastic flow*). Named after Mount Pelée on the island of Martinique in the West Indies.

Pele's hair Golden hairlike threads of volcanically spun glass, commonly found on the ground after fire-fountain activity at Hawaiian-type eruptions; named for the hair of the Hawaiian volcano goddess Pele.

plate tectonics The theory that the earth's crust is composed of rigid plates that drift atop the more fluid upper mantle.

Plinian-type eruption Characterized by powerful explosions that continue at full force for several hours. Fantastic columns of churning ash rise to great heights. Named after Pliny the Elder of Rome who lost his life while studying the great Vesuvius eruption in A.D. 79.

pyroclastic flow An extremely dangerous eruption of hot volcanic ash and debris that charges downslope like an avalanche, incinerating everything in its path. It forms out of the failure of a vertical ash column or the frontal collapse of an active lava *dome*. Also called *nuée ardente*.

rhyolite A light volcanic rock with an average *silica* content of 73 percent. When molten its *viscosity* is extremely high.

rift zone A highly fractured region extending radially from the summit of a volcano. Frequently the site of eruptive activity.

shield volcano A volcano with gently sloping sides, created from eruptions of fluid lavas onto its summit and slopes.

silica A molecule of silicon and oxygen (SiO_2) that is the principal ingredient of volcanic rock. The amount of silica in molten rock also controls its fluidity; the higher the silica content, the greater the *viscosity*.

skylight A hole in the ceiling over an active *lava tube*.

spatter Pasty globs of molten lava spit out of a *vent* with little force. The accumulation of spatter around the vent can form a spatter cone. A large spatter cone is called a *hornito*.

stratovolcano See *composite volcano*.

Strombolian-type eruption Characterized by periodic, sudden gas explosions that shoot out lava and volcanic fragments with tremendous force. Lava flows associated with such activity are predominantly basaltic to andesitic. Named after Stromboli, a volcanic island off the coast of Italy.

subduction-type volcano A volcano that occurs on the continental side of a deep-sea trench at a *subduction zone*.

subduction zone The area where two tectonic plates collide, and one slips beneath the other, forming a deep trench at the plates' boundary.

vent The opening through which a volcano erupts lava and ash.

viscosity A measure of a fluid's resistance to flow.

Vulcanian-type eruption Characterized by the violent explosion of viscous lava that creates a kilometers-high, roiling ash cloud. Thick, sluggish flows of viscous lava usually ooze out of the vent after the initial explosion. Named after Vulcano, a volcanic island off the coast of Sicily.

SUGGESTED READING

Bird, Isabella L. *Six Months in the Sandwich Islands.* Charles E. Tuttle Co., Inc., 1974.

Day, A. Grove, ed. *Mark Twain's Letters from Hawaii.* University of Hawaii Press, 1966.

Decker, Robert W., and Decker, Barbara B. *Mountains of Fire: The Nature of Volcanoes.* Cambridge University Press, 1991.

Francis, Peter. *Volcanoes.* Penguin Books, Ltd., 1976.

Frierson, Pamela. *The Burning Island: A Journey Through Myth and History in Volcano Country, Hawai'i.* Sierra Club Books, 1991.

Krafft, Maurice. *Volcanoes: Fire from the Earth.* Harry N. Abrams, Inc., 1993.

Macdonald, Gordon A.; Abbott, Agatin T.; and Peterson, Frank L. *Volcanoes in the Sea: The Geology of Hawaii,* 2nd ed. University of Hawaii Press, 1983.

Ollier, Cliff. *Volcanoes.* Basil Blackwell, Inc., 1988.

Tazieff, Haroun. *Craters of Fire.* Harper & Brothers, 1952.

Weisel, Dorian, and Heliker, Christina. *Kilauea: The Newest Land on Earth.* Bishop Museum Press, 1990.

Westervelt, W. D. *Myths and Legends of Hawaii.* Mutual Publishing Co., 1987.

For Monthly Information About Erupting Volcanoes:

Smithsonian Institution. *Bulletin* of the Global Volcanism Network, National Museum of Natural History, MRC 129, Washington, D. C. 20560.

ON DECEMBER 15, 1991, MOUNT ETNA, EUROPE'S TALLEST AND MOST ACTIVE VOLCANO, BEGAN ITS 10TH MAJOR ERUPTION THIS CENTURY AND THE LARGEST IN THE LAST 300 YEARS. THREE WEEKS LATER, THE MOUNTAIN'S WEST WALL RIPS OPEN, LETTING LAVA BLEED ONTO THE FLOOR OF VALLE DEL BOVE. FOR 6.4 KILOMETERS THE RIVERS OF FIRE BRANCH AND JOIN. IT IS AN INDECISIVE FLOW OF MOLTEN ROCK ON A JOURNEY HEADING DANGEROUSLY CLOSE TO POPULATED REGIONS. THE CITY LIGHTS OF FORNAZZO GLITTER ANXIOUSLY IN THE DISTANCE. THE ERUPTION LASTS 473 DAYS AND COVERS ABOUT 7 SQUARE KILOMETERS OF LAND WITH MORE THAN 250 MILLION CUBIC METERS OF LAVA. (SICILY)